Source

Source

Poems by *FRED CHAPPELL*

Louisiana State University Press
Baton Rouge and London
1985

for
Heath
and
Katha

Designer: Christopher Wilcox
Typeface: Times
Typesetter: Moran Colorgraphic

Library of Congress Cataloging in Publication Data

Chappell, Fred, 1936-
  Source.
  I. Title.
PS3553.H298S68   1985   811'.54   85-13315
ISBN 0-8071-1276-3
ISBN 0-8071-1277-1 (pbk.)

Publication of this book has been supported by a grant from the National Endow-
ment for the Arts in Washington, D.C., a federal agency.

Some of these poems first appeared in *Abatis One, Appalachian Journal, Back Door,
Brown Bag, Carolina Quarterly, Chattahoochee Review, Davidson Miscellany,*
Greensboro *Sun, Hemlocks & Balsams, Hollow Spring Review of Poetry, Light
Years, Plainsong, Ploughshares, Poetry, Sewanee Review, Small Farm, Southern
Humanities Review, Southern Poetry Review,* and *Touchstone.*

"The Virtues," "Recovery of Sexual Desire," "Music as Natural Resource,"
"Music as a Woman Imperfectly Perceived," and "Awakening to Music" were
published in *Awakening to Music*, Briarpatch Press, Davidson, N.C.

"Seated Figure" was published in *The World Between the Eyes*, Louisiana State
University Press.

Contents

Child in the Fog

Sir, the worst way of being intimate, is by scribbling.

—Dr. Johnson

Child in the Fog

Did the ghosts watch my prayers when the strange
Fat hats of everything attacked?
Or was it the fearful Nobody?
From the silent creek, glories of wet gauze.
The pigeons curled up in fists and mourned to me.

I began to know how
The Hour Without Eyes is gathering in the world.

The barn's hard lines went soft; rafters
Dissolved to spirit; the mice in the loft
Mumbled warm dreams.
The gray tin roof wept an old woman's tears.

This was the rapture of humility which kept saying,
You are a child, you are suitable to be awed.
I heard the whole silence.
My heart went white.

It was the first day of school and Mama
Had betrayed me to the white fog leopard,
Tree-croucher to eat my bones.
I crept to first grade like an opossum.
Afterward, the fog was my comforting cool sleep;
I could walk unseeable.
Not even the ghosts could be sure where I'd been.

Today I will build a fire the fog will clasp.
Childhood will burn in the grate and the white smoke
Will go out friendly to the white world.
All that I feared will attenuate in air,
Muffling in hush the dripping hills,
And the other lost children, and the one lost child.

Nocturne

The black horse lifts its head and quivers
Its glossy shoulder. Powder of stars
Upon the autumn sky. A wind
Springs up and slides gray walnut branches
Across the primitive constellation.
An emery of frost on the slant fields.

An old man trudges the midnight road,
Bearing a totesack over his shoulder,
Bearing away in steady silence
All the breath of country sleepers.
Something small and trembling emerges
From the pond and seeks its leaf-warm burrow.
The stars creep back over the water.

And then the
one
bellchime of moonrise.

A Prayer for Slowness

Let the deep valley take me over
with its sundown shadow a little at a time,
by little and little, as if the hourglass
lay on its side and the grains leaked through
one by one into the cloud of infinite separate
moments. I shall enter that cloud

when once I am become as slow as the brindle
cow who walks the molded path along the hill
to shadow of the barn darker than hill shadow,
not lifting her broad head to watch the climb of
spade-edge shadow on the other mountain, but
steadily imprinting the dust with her divided name,

going into the barn where her rich welcome
is taken from her, to lie down grateful and eased.

Let the
find the
from sto
headlong

He shall kn
He shall per
Let the poem
it can be igno

I have come to
and turned back
in breathy twiligh

illumines my hands
fails in my hands lik
Let the poem say its

H

Burdened with d
Queen Anne's la
The lace is full
That draw a co
The ditch twin
And the groun
With little hol
Where his bl

6

7

adem, the
ce overhangs the ditch.
f eyes, cold eyes
d sky into their spheres.
kles now the rain has stopped.
d begins to puff and suck
es. A man could live down here forever,
od is.

A Prayer for the Mountains

Let these peaks have happened.

The hawk-haunted knobs and hollers,
The blind coves, blind as meditation, the white
Rock-face, the laurel hells, the terraced pasture ridge
With its broom sedge combed back by wind:
Let these have taken place, let them be place.

And where Rich Fork drops uprushing against
Its tabled stones, let the gray trout
Idle below, its dim plectrum a shadow
That marks the stone's clear shadow.

In the slow glade where sunlight comes through
In circlets and moves from leaf to fallen leaf
Like a tribe of shining bees, let
The milk-flecked fawn lie unseen, unfearing.

Let me lie there too and share the sleep
Of the cool ground's mildest children.

Humility

In the necessary field among the round
Warm stones we bend to our gleaning.
The brown earth gives in to our hands, and straw
By straw burns red aslant the vesper light.

The village behind the graveyard tolls softly, begins
To glow with new-laid fires. The children
Quiet their shouting, and the martins slide
Above the cows at the warped pasture gate.

They set the tinware out on checkered oilcloth
And the thick-mouthed tumblers on the right-hand side.
The youngest boy whistles the collie to his dish
And lifts down the dented milk pail:

This is the country we return to when
For a moment we forget ourselves,
When we watch the sleeping kitten quiver
After long play, or rain comes down warm.

Here we might choose to live always, here where
Ugly rumors of ourselves do not reach,
Where in the whisper-light of the kerosene lamp
The deep Bible lies open like a turned-down bed.

Awakening to Music

I don't forget head down
striding the raw ridges, snowbit,
knuckles red burning knots of ice
in my pockets, wind turning funnels of snow-snuff,
and cursing as I bulled along
a whiteface heifer who must have daintily
tiptoed through
the curlicues of busted barbwire
and loped excited away in sparkling cold
to skirmish my father's neighbors' fields
or maybe the whole wide silly world
in a sharp wind getting sharper always
at the awkward hour, dawn
bleaching to ash or dark coming on with
no one abroad to ask of
about stray cows.

    Till finally we met.
This coquette, tossing her rag-curled
forehead, tossing the silky string
of lucid snot pearly from chin to knees
like a Charleston necklace.
                  "Come home now,
Daisy''; and she'd ballhoot
the rocky road with a racket like a marble
rolling down a washboard, leaving
a breath-white ghost I blinked at.

I'd curse to melt the snow in air.

Sometimes:
        with hands frost-grained
from the bucket bail I'd clutch the brood-warm
teats and God help us how she'd kick a shapely
leg as sudden as a door blown shut.
Or just as quick in August when
thistle-thorns embedded in the udders.

Sickness worst of all.
The little Jersey down in the smelly straw,
eyes back, brown eyes enfolding flame-blue
eggs in the light of a Coleman fizzing
like seltzer, and Doc McGreavy lying down
in warm embrace, ear
to guttering lungs, choosing without having to look
the iron and glass in the lumpy black bag.
The terrible births: my throat wire-taut,
hands stiff, while Doc plunged shoulder-deep
in flesh-muck, a one-armed swimmer.

Yet even so the main thing:
was every morning the cuddling when my head
went into her toasty flank, the grandest magic helmet
breathing and her red belly
rubbing my intimate right shoulder,
and milk-squirt slicing through the foam
like yard on yard of brocade piling up.

That was how I came from sleep to another sleep,
came into a warm swamp-broad sleep,
warm rain on heart-shaped leaves and dozing orchids,
came to the pulsing green fountain where music is born.

And all those years I went clothed in this sleep,
odor and warmth
of cows blanketed about my head.

How would I get it back? Go to blood
again, sleep the light green sleep?
How can I wake, not waking to music?

Exile

The judge aloft in his howdah
on the elephant Authority
sways. Like a golden scab
the Seal of State glows in the
courtroom. The prisoner
whispers like a small dry wind.
"I was innocent once,
I was a child. My innocence
died. Is there no compassion
for one whose innocence died?"

Exile is the judge's sentence;
and they confiscate the childhood.

Abandoned Schoolhouse
on Long Branch

The final scholar scrawls his long
Black name in aisle dust, licks the air
With his tendril double tongue,
Coils up in shadow of a busted chair

And dozes like the farmer boys
Who never got straight the capital
Of Idaho, found out the joys
Of long division, or learned what all

Those books were all about. Most panes
Are gone now and the web-milky windows
Are open to the world. Gold dust-grains
Swirl up, and show which way the wind blows.

K.B. + R.J., cut deep
In a darkened heart on the cloakroom wall.
Now Katherine Johnson and Roger sleep
Quite past the summons of the morning bell.

The teacher sleeps narrow too, on yonder
Side of Sterling Mountain, as stern
With her grave as with a loutish blunder
In the Bible verse she set them to learn.

Sunset washes the blackboard. Bees
Return to the rich attic nest
Where much is stored. Their vocalese
Entrances the native tranquil dust.

Seated Figure

Immense blind wind marching the grove,
Mauling the stolid house, and thrusting
Its paw down the torn flue. The stove
Roared, stuffed with flame to bursting.

The darkened mother crouched to her needle.
Her rocking chair tipped back and forth.
Slowly the house began to sidle
In the bare wind scouring the dim earth.

Even when blue snow swarmed fast
Against the pane and light went glass-gray
She gave no sign. Time was past
She took notice of wind-fray.

The night hurtled upon the night.
The roof groaned; arose; then gone,
Like an owl tumbling the spare light.
She drove her needle under the bone moon.

TWO   *Source*

A louse and a flea kept house together and were brewing beer in an egg-shell.

—Grimm's Fairy Tales

The Evening of the Second Day

I

What can remain but exile striking the frozen door
What can remain but hunger and yammer and trembling
What can be felt but despair of returning
What can be seen but sacred fields in ashes

II

Vault of the olive in ruin
and the choked spring rust-colored with discarded plunder

Teeth and bone shards the gravedigger's hoe turns up
and cattle refusing to come down to the river
and bat-spattered shell casings stacked in the barn loft

The only green things the scattered bales of money

Maybe six feet under the city a newspaper is found unburned
with the politician intact with his pottery grin,
another powerless totem we toss aside
for our cubs to scrap over

The skies now and then
whistling with uncontrolled missiles
Horizon now and then blue-white
with unexplained detonation
withers our fearful half-sleep
Magenta fire dances on the craters

At twilight while the females groom for lice
we stare at our hands, at the cracked caked nails
and croon wordless lullabyes until we cough

III

After the last salvo of broken gas main
After the strategic attack of the rats
After your sister on all fours has died fearing water
After your father's grave goes up in the minefield
your head grows hotter, you see only a sliding mist

After searching the midden for edible grubs
how will you call death peace,
so long living in death without respite

IV

Today we marched two miles east to avoid
a shadow whose shape we did not understand
Tomorrow we will huddle under the glowing mountain

On this migration the food is scarce and weevil-eaten
The young are blue and whimpering
We might have stayed to fight the Big Head People

With the Big Heads we have already fought and lost
and with the One Eyes
with the People Not Speaking and with the Screechers
with the Chewers of Knives and the Blotch Faces
with the Puddlers and Kneewalkers and the Poison Hand People
with the Wallowdogs and the People Who Crawl in Shit
We have battled and been driven out in pain

V

Today Mushgut found evidence we are being followed
and late afternoon we heard the ravine scramble and snicker
When we came to the waterhole a blood-daubed effigy
stood propped with broken rock
and Shudderfoot saw it and ran away to weep

No one believes we are near the place we promised ourselves

VI

I for one no longer watch the discolored stars
When Blindboy reads the entrails of birds I stop my ears
I do not care that they cast the oracular knuckles
All these measures are tardy and heartsick

Time now to choose one of us for stoning

The Lost Carnival

I

She feels her presence as never
before, here where the dim little carnival
departs. Where she is never
following, never, never.

The young girl stands at the circle of beaten ground.
Sparrows and starlings peckpeck
the stale confetti bits of popcorn.
On the power pole crossbar
a big crow hunches his shoulders.

II

She remembers the shouts of brass, the razzle-dazzle
festoons, the candy butcher's red tattoo,
AMERICA. But nothing was ever sadder
than the carousel unicorn's chipped nose
and how the Ferris wheel rattled its gondolas in wind.

III

Where has the little carnival gone?
She imagines a blizzard mountain pass,
the elephants trumpeting in snow, the acrobats
shouldering the mired wagons.
The restless tigers pad through the falling flakes.

19

Music as a Woman
Imperfectly Perceived

1

Felt in air touchless not merely
      as noon light is touchless, impalpable
      yet rounded still and whole, but
in air existing and just now coming to exist,

as in a fog-quiet autumn dawn the three low
      dew-cool notes of the mourning dove
      across mist-washed grass and fence wire
suffuse themselves to hearing.

As in a strange old house a dimness
discovered between the wall and eye's striving,
      and a murmurous scent
      of wilted perfume and stiff linen.

So this woman not quite before us: the way
when walking seaward we hear by little and little
the lace edge of its sluicing never receding.

Listening becomes a quality that shears off
in great blue mirrors, chasm against chasm
of silvered blue, an endless falling.

2

Is this the real substance of purgatory?
This is the shadow-kingdom, unblemished globe of discretions.

Does the woman inhabit these seamless corridors?
Here the Queen of Intimations goes walking.

What other animals here?
Dragonflies peel up the skins of space like carpenter's planes.

In what form shall we seek that woman?
Whatever paradigm brightness best cleaves to.

What clothing is worn in this azure country?
Gossamer and armor.

Will anyone here understand our tongue?
So well indeed that you cannot lie.

From point to point, how far?
Rainbow-piers are your distance markers.

Are there many great dangers?
You will tremble but not in fear.

Can we return alive?
Alive, but not unchanged.

3

    Came tooling my blue canoe by the flute zoo & could
hear the guys smelting new sound from the raw ore. Struck
sparks aloft in the dark & whimpering glimmer of slim
strings. Sez to myself, What they up to now? Always
carrying on to beat the band. But I couldn't tell nothing
yet, the way it was mutey and murky, so I spunked the
hulk onto the bank midst the sassy grasses & just laid
back there to see what I could spy, feeling like something
bound to come down. Long time though they just tuning the
bones, *boom bang & burp*, while I laid with my patience.
Hard now & then to tell when they *do* begin, oboe trooping
down like a doe shy to the slow stream, maniacal cackle
of the snare full of grackles, snoopy swoop of the hambone
trombone, & so forth. You been here, you know how I mean.
You know in your blood, they going to start to stump it.
Mud thud as the bass drum chomps its cud, then they all go
hush as feathers except the kettle man still bobbling his
knobs. Just waiting . . . What a sight in the bright, all that
noise poised.
    Now.
    Comes down tiptoe like mice stacking poker chips, the
air full of careful, & they needling in place the lace
cerise. But suddenly dump it bubbling out, washtub of ticklish
champagne. Trumpets climb ladders with teeth out, French
horns shelving the staves bungshut. The fiddles keep trading
trousers, every tweedle is a riddle. Now back again to chipping
dimes with silver hammers. Hello cello. The double basses
cuddle the funk like four mules in a furrow. These here

barhoppers go whooping up the line, sharing their woes and
showing their wares. Is everybody crazy yet? Why not, like to
know. The bully brass will slice your ass. I'm going down
where the tall reeds grow. I want to hear the clarinets come
down for a drink of spring water & the flutes splash stars
on a sea of quicksilver. I want to see the bassoon tumble
down the stairs, hurtle-turtle and gaudy mahogany. I hear
the harp plucking lint off her evening gown, piano spitting
big gooey gobs of taffy, the organ bawling out the sweaty
elephant drovers. Swear the tuba's gonna lay a bowling ball
and set there till it hatches. Even the steel chairs are
alert and throbbing like tombstones.

Those boys were *bad*, I mean, like, *good*. Who this dude
Mo-zart is? Anyhow?

4

My love smiles brightly on the silver glass,
And the winds fly down with the sighing clock singing.
All that she wondered has come to pass,
And she flows into air like the white bird winging
Away, away,
To yesterday,
Where lilies and roses clean whiteness come bringing.
She sheds such grace
Upon this place
Of darkness, that every flower burns brightly in her face.

Music as Natural Resource

Great carpets of it, as far as you could see.
Savage green savannas, wild uplands of music
where concertos grazed in peace
and the grand operas battled shaggy in mating season
under the stolid mountains.
Symphonies raged in the mouths of rivers.
Tip to trembling tip,
flutes and harps and clarinets scampered the tree limbs,
gossiping like fugues.
This was before progress got here.

Then they laid the track.
Buddy Bolden drove that golden spike.

Now this whole country is nothing but haul-ass
from dawn to dawn.
Somebody I tell you is going crazy.
Go get em, Yardbird. Git it on.

23

Transmogrification of the Diva

May she lie sleeping still
While the well-mannered dust powders the frayed
Pink prissy ribbons adrift on mother-of-pearl.
The elderly cat at bedfoot dozes, his eyes
Plump-shut with drowse. She will not longingly stir,
Half-open hands at peace.

Keep the squabbles of tenors
Far now from her whole rest; let the curtain rise
Over the pit, floodlight knifing above
The horns and varnished oboes; let maestro
Carve the unfathomable score, while she
In-breathes the musk of time.

Let the listeners yet crave
Her ghost-glimmer in the second act:
That sweet note the young soprano cannot form.
May it then transpire: pure clean shaft
Of music open her breast to the gilded trompe l'oeil
Skies where the rich swans stream.

Latencies

First point of light and then another and another: the stars
come out, bright fishnet lifting from darkness those broken
many heroes we read the mind with.
This is the notion of *latencies* I partly drew from books.

Suppose there is no present time, only the latent past: a trout
rising to noon river's surface reinstates the dawn,
whiff of it here where I tie on the Adams. The trout is silent,
he is a latent prayer, I cannot entice him to say so.

The woman stands by the window, strikes a posture
that suddenly recalls to me a decade of obliterate dreams.
The window is a latent religion. Thrust it open, and
what new knowledge, new immanence, pour in upon us.

Or consider the young man fishing the river. Now he
has gone to be a soldier, he has become
a latent garden of terrible American Beauty roses
which only the enemy bullets can make manifest.

The Story

Once upon a time the farmer's wife
told it to her children while she scrubbed potatoes.
There were wise ravens in it, and a witch
who flew into such a rage she turned to brass.

The story wandered about the countryside until
adopted by the palace waiting maids
who endowed it with three magic golden rings
and a handsome prince named Felix.

Now it had both strength and style and visited
the household of the jolly merchant
where it was seated by the fire and given
a fat gray goose and a comic chambermaid.

One day alas the story got drunk and fell
in with a crowd of dissolute poets.
They drenched it with moonlight and fever and fed it
words from which it never quite recovered.

Then it was old and haggard and disreputable,
carousing late at night with defrocked scholars
and the swaggering sailors in Rattlebone Alley.
That's where the novelists found it.

Fox and Goose

Fox took him a yearn for honey.
Paced up & down his nervous den pitpat.
He went outside.
It was a moonlit night.
   O the moon the moon-O
   Above the frosty hill.

He came to the hive where the bees were sleeping,
Snoring like a string quintet.
And here was Goose marching his sentry circuit.

Fox thought it wise to soothe and flatter.
"Hello, Handsome, what say we go for a little walk?
I got a song to sing you.
I got a tale to tell."

But Goose was not so silly as the name they gave him.
Quick quick he hollered up the bulldog Ugly.
Ugly bit Fox right to death.

But this was never the end of Fox, no children no.
His soul rose growling beyond the moon unsatisfied.

And that is why we see among the stars
The constellation named *The Fox Forestalled*
That only comes out on moonlit nights
When the honey is young and sweet.

Establish

Establish
the other race of beings. The harps
of the lissome willows curtain
the roadside where the children
play with the fingers
of the soldier's corpse.

Perched on his ravaged chest
like sparrows, they sing and chatter.
The moon is a dish of frost,
the roosting stars coo and flutter
as the gray fox traipses daintily
past the charred city.

Trolls

In the land beyond Vimur
the trolls deceived you. That door
you could not shut was, in reality,
Remorse, which has no quit.
The knot too complex to untie
was Time; the fire that gave no light
was Pain-of-Children.

Then they worked their final joke
and made you your father's son.

Silent

In Hela's hall bright Baldur
and dark Honur sit. No word
is said or need be said.
They are content. The death,
the mistletoe arrow,
are buried in time.

New snow invests that memory
with a quiet dignity.
Fimbul Winter casts its sleep
on all but the veering blackbird
whose little scythe scores deep
across the silent wood.

Narcissus and Echo

Shall the water not remember   *Ember*
my hand's slow gesture, tracing above   *of*
its mirror my half-imaginary   *airy*
portrait? My only belonging   *longing*;
is my beauty, which I take   *ache*
away and then return, as love   *of*
teasing playfully the one being   *unbeing.*
whose gratitude I treasure   *Is your*
moves me. I live apart   *heart*
from myself, yet cannot   *not*
live apart. In the water's tone,   *stone?*
that brilliant silence, a flower   *Hour,*
whispers my name with such slight   *light*:
moment, it seems filament of air,   *fare*
the world become cloudswell.   *well.*

Charge

Black pyramid of cannonballs
by the pediment are turds
of the bronze horse the general
steadfastly sits like a spike
driven into a brain. The words
the general spoke lie in a book,
his pointing sword
directs an army of clouds.

Recovery of Sexual Desire
After a Bad Cold

Toward morning I dreamed of the Ace of Spades reversed
And woke up giggling.
New presence in the bedroom, as if it had snowed;
And an obdurate stranger come to visit my body.

This is how it all renews itself, floating down
Mothy on the shallow end of sleep;
How Easter gets here, and the hard-bitten dogwood
Flowers, and waters run clean again.

I am a new old man.
As morning sweetens the forsythia and the cats
Bristle with impudent hungers, I learn to smile.
I am a new baby.

What woman could turn from me now?
Shining like a butter knife, and the fever burned off,
My whole skin alert as radar, I can think
Of nothing at all but love and fresh coffee.

Rib

I have taken the rib of a woman
and fashioned a hazelnut.
Inside it lives an elfin
cobbler whose delight
is carving tiny women from bone.

In April the shell breaks open
and the women all fly out
in a swarm of breathless shine
to infest the sleepy roses
of the temperate zone.

The Virtues

The vices are always hungry for my hands,
But the virtues stay inside their houses like shy brown thrushes.

I feel their presences
Behind the white clapboard walls with all the ugly gingerbread.

They are walking about the dim cool rooms
In handsewn linen dresses.

Is it empty to wish they will come out
To sweep the walks when I stand under the oak across the street?

The virtues are widowed sisters.
No man has been with them for many years.

I believe they are waiting for cataclysm.
They will open their doors

When perfect ruin has taken down this city,
Will wander forth and sift thoughtfully in the hot rubble.

Source

An ancient wound troubles the river
where the horses drink their reed-spiked shadows.
The perfumed barge drifts by, bearing
a final viceroy to oblivion.
Far lamentation of lacquered courtesans
swells in the breeze like echo of a cloud.

The gray-eyed peasant
leans on his scythe, the barge enters his reverie
and noses toward the source of twilight,
the source of ravens. A bell has spoken once only,
then that long tower of sound wavers and dissolves.

THREE

The Transformed Twilight

a lieder cycle

The Transformed Twilight

1

The night wind billows these volumes of silk,
Veils of melancholy water where suspend
The worlds in agate flame like childhood tears.
We wander the woman whose tresses devour our small mystery.

A mountain of darkness. Moon gnaws its shoulder.
Where does desire discover the shoal of satin light?
The mountain like a metropolis of light illuminates
An incurable tombstone awaiting its ordained name.

Your little hands, dear love, are the moon's white ferrets.
Our bed undulant in the black ocean mirror,
The canopy swarms with tradewind, Polaris unfixed
And dropping toward the planet's unsteady margin.

2

The sculptor walks at twilight into the grove
Where gray shadows trouble the torso
His half-sleep has polished, sardonic double light
Of flesh and marble beneath the stone flame of Hesperus.

The flesh of whitened shadow arises from shadow,
A smoke of light substantial as delirium.
Torment torment of being flesh,
Of not being flesh. Pact with unbroken eternity.

What firm rage instructs this skillful history?
You, love, are emerging into time, anxieties
Of motion. You, love, with your embattled poise,
Absorb the uncertainties of the pale half-risen moon.

3

Gash the starlost head till it bleed light.
Now you are crazy, that is the world's letter
To me . . . And so I wend the meadow
To where the shepherds flaunt their sonnets,

To where the Fragonard distance melts in longing;
Verlaine, and all the pastoral others . . .
Then the intoxication of speed and disaster,
I am hurtling wild centuries of blind savor,

Pour of wilderness horizon, pure cataracts of time.
The head holds back its shriek, hysteria
Begins its ponderous working like a heavy truck
Straining uphill with a cargo of embalmed fathers.

4

That was fine yes that was all very fine,
Not only the torture and maiming, but the colonel's
Eagle buttons that gleamed like plasma packs
And the boots waiting for their feet to be extracted like teeth.

No one asked about the children but someone felt good
About the whole thing, as if it were finished long ago
And in the books. You told me you had a vision
Of all the world naked at once, and everyone old.

Everyone seventy years old, and bringing to the helicopter
Ears and fingers as trophies, little rancid cigars
Strung round their withered necks, and in the evening
We drank sake and that was fine, that was very good.

5

I am shuddering now, don't ask me why, keep your hands,
Your little white hands, please, there, yes right there.
Villages of children lift their ruined faces in the bedsheet.
Now turn this way, maybe we will not dream tonight.

I can imagine no brutal history that will not be born,
Each crude suffering will stay till daylight.
The implacable foreign stars hang crooked with dew
Until the sudden round of alien dawn fires them phosphor.

I need to remember the names of your hands,
So many times glowing in vision before me
In the nighttime while I heard the perimeter
Gather its furtive rustlings into one black terror.

6

The forms I sculpt I have dragged out of shadow
That holds a shifting light intermittent
With blurred faces. Was there really something there?
A man will turn to another man to ask what he saw.

I reach into the crumbled centuries and draw forth cherubs,
Nymphs, and pediments, which do not overpower
The chopper's throaty throb and the bamboo
Straining back away and the white grass warped down

Where the stretcher-bearers trotted stooped.
Today and tomorrow depart like cloud
And will not give over into stone. The ineffable forms
Escape my hand, my hand the chisel of shadow.

7

Let our whole history come then to this:
That your slim white hands have smoothed my thigh
While Sirius flew up incandescent like a mortar flare
And night whirled round the horizon like carousel bunting.

Many certain things have come unbolted and drift
In capsized cloud or upon the world's slow barcarole surface,
Nudging and thumping together until at last
Their names flake and slough off in ragged flags.

I have imagined the stars in clean white rows.
That was strict insanity. Now they commingle with flesh
And shadow and stone and breath, a nebula
Of accident I thrust my hand into until it vanishes.

FOUR

Forever Mountain

To dwellers in a wood almost every species of tree has its voice as well as its feature.

—Thomas Hardy

The Capacity for Pain

I am changing shape again.

After the sleepless decades, after the violent transformations,
The numb debaucheries,
The groveling on hands and knees,
I begin to tense toward dimmer forms:
Bat and slug, mole, gray louse, alley rat.

In currents of darkling wind, voices whimper
To me; words are wandering here, each of them
Takes on an ugly fur.
I cannot abide these words in my mouth.

Whatever detritus the troopers' boots grind down,
I will eat that. Whether it is tatters
Of holy books or the torn blood of children,
I will eat that.
I want to understand civilization.

Windows

For Anne Newman

                              Such
the nature of this darkness each
death
is a window. Every death lets in
gray light. To look about us, recognize
the terrors one by one. We are grateful
for these windows diminishing our company
one by one. What is the source of this light,

this death? In the long dark warehouse
there is no window until someone dies.
Now we know
we inhabit human company, the gray
light steals across the unforgiving vacancy,
the tired source of death is that impervious space
between galaxies. Each face lifted
to a new window with the expression of someone
suddenly struck deaf.   Still

it is true, we had to learn the terrors here, we
had to know. The light of many deaths gives us
our bearings, but

                    now,
too many deaths, the light grows whiter, we
have become a brotherhood who were only
a crowd of strangers. A new order,
is it? Is this the new order always promised?

Or: this mealy light the afterglow of the giant
death of some far legendary sun. The light
at any rate is growing, more deaths identify
themselves.

We turn away from one
another nauseated, what sad result of truth.
We huddle into ourselves. Beaten by
obscure longings.
                    The light keeps growing
like a snowdrift, we cannot evade the windows.

And the prayed-for transformation
remains stone.

Afterseasons, Countershades

1

Butcher, cut me down.

The gallows creak and straighten again
As my weight swings out, lengthening
Over the alien ground the saints sleep in.
My shadow fractures.

The far-off echo of my whimpered good-bye
Is lost among the pendulum stones.
The stones are saying farewell,
They will eat no more my shadow.
A final lantern sways before me,
A premonitory Hesperus.

2

Uncertainly trudging uncertain terrain.

Beneath the ocean pour of oak leaves, I walk
Like a diver among the sunken logs;
The wattles of ivory soften like the meats
Of drowned sailors.

Path to the luckless heart of this planet unmarked,
No matter how many have gone before.
The surface of shadow reflects my hand.

3

Friends, you have gone with me as far as you may.
When I look back, you seem to regard me
With steady regret. *As far as you may.*
Then scimitar darkness overtakes my journey.

4

But that was all so long ago, wasn't it long ago?

I felt my death as a tremor over a still pond,
The trembling a cloud might make, raking
The black surface.

51

The seasons trail through decaying plains.

Bemused, as if by a distant symphony.

A sojourner's grave is narrower than he could have thought.

I lie down faithful to wait the hopeless advent.
I have lapped like a dog the shallows of eternity.

Urleid

I

All that forever is scattered from a man.
Home no more at twilight to set his sandals
Side by side on the hearth and hug his children.
Forever changes everything:

He is folded into another being, a tree perhaps.
The atoms that were his mind far-sprinkled
In space, his life a banquet of snow for sun.
The wolves tear his body or cold stone oppresses,

And he cannot look back. The embalmer with
His sanctimonious honey, his weeping wife,
The priest with slow hand gestures
Tracing his luckless destiny, so what?

II

Lucretius said:
"The detestable Rilke: those angels, star-tangled
Trees, countesses with pale hands. Images
That helpless fancy creates, they burn
And yet remain, teasing the mind to frenzy.
It is no honey nymph you take to bed but
A ghost whose lips you bite to blood,
The sexy sweats of the body like dew on a tombstone.

"The silliest movie is that empty drawing-room farce
They call Olympus. The leisure class perches
Its porcelain villa on the shale edge of void.
They faintly hear the roaring."

III

And said again:
"The comfort is, there's nothing personal in it.
The seeds of things put forth foreordained fruit,
Nothing's wasted, nothing crazy, nothing
Out of nowhere to attack a man for nothing.

"Trust Venus as she entices Mars, as
She leans over his gleaming swaggerstick,
Her hair down, bright along her flanks. Her lips
Breathe in his unsteady breath, her cool hands
Undo the careful buttons."

IV

Lucretius has walked out far to view the Gorgon
Terror. Returned to shape
His thoughts and suffer the windburn histories
Of city and animal and star.
His hand is pure and alone.

We saw you in the white fountain of delirium
Burning but not purified.

Message
For David Slavitt

True.

    The first messenger angel may arrive
purely clothed in terror, the form he takes
a swordblade of unbearable energies, making
the air he entered a spice of ozone.

And then, the mad inventories. Each force
of nature, each animal and pretty bird,
is guilty with persistence. The tear of sorrow,
huge as an alien star, invades
our sun's little system.

                    Irrelevant,
such enormity: because the man is alone
and naked. Even the tenuous radiations
of the marauding star crush him like falling timbers.
The worst is, he must choose among sorrows
the one that destroys him most.

                    But see how all
changes in that hour. He ascends
a finer dimension of event, he feels with senses
newly evolved the wide horizons unknown till now.
He is transformed head to foot, taproot to polestar.
He breathes a new universe, the blinding whirlpool
galaxies drift round him and begin to converse.

O Sacred Head Now Wounded

The hundred staring doors.
The maddened crows, crown
Of daggerthorn. The savage town
Burning alive, the savage stars.

And on the road, blood
Weeping and shrieking like bone.
The whipped man standing alone
Where no man ever stood.

Faces like rancid pockets.
Broken teeth clawing beard
And snarl-curled lip. Heads blurred
With wine. The worms sniggering in the eyesockets.

Forever Mountain
J. T. Chappell, 1912–1978

Now a lofty smoke has cleansed my vision.

I see my father has gone to climb
Easily the Pisgah slope, taking the time
He's got a world of, making spry headway
In the fresh green mornings, stretching out
Noontimes in the groves of beech and oak.
He has cut a walking stick of second-growth hickory
And through the amber afternoon he measures
Its shadow and his own shadow on a sunny rock.
        Not marking the hour, but observing
The quality of light come over him.
He is alone, except what voices out of time
Come to his head like bees to the bee-tree crown,
The voices of former life as indistinct as heat.

By the clear trout pool he builds his fire at twilight,
And in the night a granary of stars
Rises in the water and spreads from edge to edge.
He sleeps, to dream the tossing dream
Of the horses of pine trees, their shoulders
Twisting like silk ribbon in the breeze.

He rises glad and early and goes his way,
Taking by plateaus the mountain that possesses him.

My vision blurs blue with distance,
I see no more.
Forever Mountain has become a cloud
That light turns gold, that wind dislimns.

        This is a prayer.